COMPARING
ANIMAL TRAITS

PILEATED WOODPECKERS

INSECT-HUNTING BIRDS

LAURA HAMILTON WAXMAN

Lerner Publications ◆ Minneapolis

For Caleb, a drummer worthy of the woodpecker

Lerner Publications Company
A division of Lerner Publishing Group, Inc.
241 First Avenue North
Minneapolis, MN 55401 USA

For reading levels and more information, look up this title at www.lernerbooks.com.

Photo Acknowledgments

The images in this book are used with the permission of: © iStockphoto.com/MartinDollenkamp, p. 1; © DickDaniels/Wikimedia Commons (CC BY-SA 3.0), p. 4; © Gerrit Vyn/Animals Animals, p. 5; © MVPhoto/ Shutterstock.com, pp. 6, 10 (left), 19; © Steve Byland/Shutterstock.com, p. 7; © Warren Price/Dreamstime. com, p. 8; © Lukas Blazek/Dreamstime.com, p. 9 (top); Larry Ditto/DanitaDelimont.com Danita Delimont Photography/Newscom, p. 9 (bottom); © Kevin Au/Shutterstock.com, p. 10 (right); © James Urbach/ SuperStock, p. 11 (left); © Ecuadorpostales/Shutterstock.com, p. 11 (right); © Laura Westlund/Independent Picture Service, p. 12; © John E Marriott/All Canada Photos/SuperStock, p. 13; © FLPA/SuperStock, p. 14; © Danita Delimont/Getty Images, p. 15; © iStockphoto.com/NNehring, p. 16; © Warren Price Photography/ Shutterstock.com, p. 17 (left); National Park Service, p. 17 (right); © iStockphoto.com/poisonsama, p. 18; © Ron Knight/Wikimedia Commons (CC BY 2.0), p. 20; © iStockphoto.com/JeffGoulden, p. 22; © Cal Vornberger/Alamy, p. 23; © McDonald Wildlife Photography/Animals Animals, pp. 24, 26; Lyle Madeson/ USDA (CC BY 2.0), p. 25; © Robert L Kothenbeutel/Shutterstock.com, p. 27 (left); © Mircea Costina/ Dreamstime.com, p. 27 (right); © Fred Whitehead/Animals Animals, p. 28; © Minden Pictures/SuperStock, p. 29.

Front cover: © Tim Zurowski/All Canada Photos/Getty Images.
Back cover: © Andrea J Smith/Shutterstock.com.

Main body text set in Calvert MT Std 12/18. Typeface provided by Monotype Typography.

Library of Congress Cataloging-in-Publication Data

Waxman, Laura Hamilton.
    Pileated woodpeckers: insect-hunting birds / Laura Hamilton Waxman.
        pages cm — (Comparing animal traits)
    Includes bibliographical references and index.
    Audience: Ages 7–10.
    Audience: Grades K to grade 3.
    ISBN 978-1-4677-9511-1 (lb : alk. paper) — ISBN 978-1-4677-9637-8 (pb : alk. paper) —
ISBN 978-1-4677-9638-5 (eb pdf)
    1. Pileated woodpecker—Juvenile literature. I. Title.
QL696.P56W39 2015
598.7'2—dc23
                                                                    2015013536

Manufactured in the United States of America
1 – BP – 12/31/15

TABLE OF CONTENTS

MEET THE PILEATED WOODPECKER

A pileated woodpecker grips the trunk of a rotting tree with its sharp, black claws. It hammers away at the wood with its beak. Pileated woodpeckers are birds. Other animal groups are fish, insects, reptiles, amphibians, and mammals.

The loud rapping of pileated woodpeckers can be heard throughout the woods where they live.

Different kinds of birds share many traits. All birds are vertebrates, which means they have backbones. They are also warm-blooded. This means their bodies make their own heat. They keep a steady temperature, even if the temperature of their surroundings changes. Most of a bird's skin is covered with feathers. All birds have two wings and a beak. Pileated woodpeckers share these characteristics with other birds. But some traits make the pileated woodpecker different from other birds.

CHAPTER 1

WHAT DO PILEATED WOODPECKERS LOOK LIKE?

Pileated woodpeckers are large, black birds. A bright red crest of feathers comes to a point on their head. White stripes zigzag down their neck. A curved line of white feathers can be seen on the underside of their wings while they are in flight.

Pileated woodpeckers are one of the world's largest woodpeckers. From beak to tail, they measure 16 to 19 inches (40 to 48 centimeters). They weigh 8.8 to 12 ounces (250 to 350 grams) and have a wingspan of 26 to 30 inches (66 to 75 cm).

DID YOU KNOW?

There are more than **180 KINDS** of woodpeckers in the world. The pileated woodpecker is the biggest woodpecker commonly seen in North America.

Pileated woodpeckers have a strong, pointy beak. They use their beak like a chisel, pecking away at wood. A pileated woodpecker hits its beak against trees up to twelve thousand times a day. A section of its skull is made of spongy bone. This bone helps absorb the impact of hitting against wood.

PILEATED WOODPECKERS VS. GREATER ROADRUNNERS

A greater roadrunner zooms through the desert as it hunts down a lizard. These speedy birds live in the southwestern United States and Mexico. Greater roadrunners share certain features with pileated woodpeckers.

From beak to tail, greater roadrunners are about 21 inches (53 cm) long. They also have a crest of feathers. They can raise and lower their black crest to scare off predators or attract mates.

A greater roadrunner runs across a desert.

Both species of birds have long beaks. Greater roadrunners use their beaks to kill prey such as snakes. Both birds also have long, stiff tail feathers. Pileated woodpeckers use their tail feathers to support their bodies against the trunks of trees. Greater roadrunners use their tail feathers for balance when running.

Both birds have feet with two toes pointing forward and two pointing back. These X-shaped feet help woodpeckers climb up trees and logs. They keep roadrunners steady as they sprint.

Greater roadrunners use their long tails to help them steer when they are running at top speeds.

DID YOU KNOW?
Greater roadrunners aren't good fliers, but they can run up to 15 MILES (24 kilometers) per hour.

PILEATED WOODPECKERS VS. AMERICAN FLAMINGOS

An American flamingo bends its long, curved neck to dip its beak into muddy water. American flamingos are much bigger than pileated woodpeckers. These flamingos are 36 to 50 inches (91 to 127 cm) tall. They can weigh 4.5 to 9 pounds (2 to 4.1 kilograms).

American flamingos are a burst of color. Their feathers are entirely pink, except for their black-tipped wings. Their legs and webbed feet are also pink. They sometimes stand on one of their long, slender legs.

The feathers of the American flamingo (*right*) are much brighter than the feathers of the pileated woodpecker.

COMPARE IT!

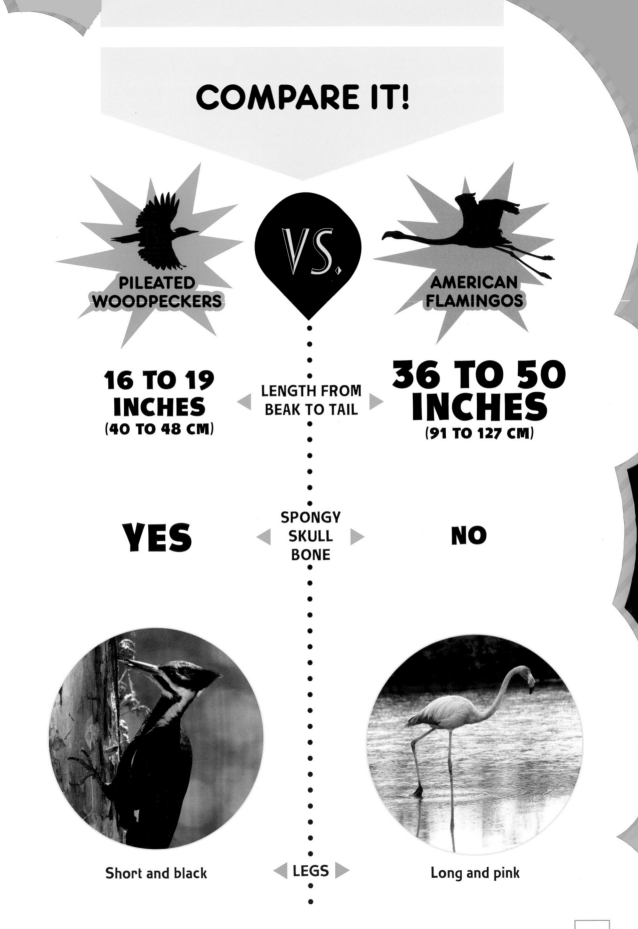

PILEATED WOODPECKERS

VS.

AMERICAN FLAMINGOS

16 TO 19 INCHES
(40 TO 48 CM)

◄ LENGTH FROM BEAK TO TAIL ►

36 TO 50 INCHES
(91 TO 127 CM)

YES

◄ SPONGY SKULL BONE ►

NO

Short and black

◄ LEGS ►

Long and pink

CHAPTER 2

WHERE DO PILEATED WOODPECKERS LIVE?

Pileated woodpeckers live in wooded habitats in the United States and Canada. They look for forests with dead and rotting trees and logs. Rotting trees are the easiest places for woodpeckers to dig out their main food, carpenter ants. They also drill for other insects burrowed into rotting wood. They feed mostly on carpenter ants and beetle larvae. They also sometimes eat berries and nuts.

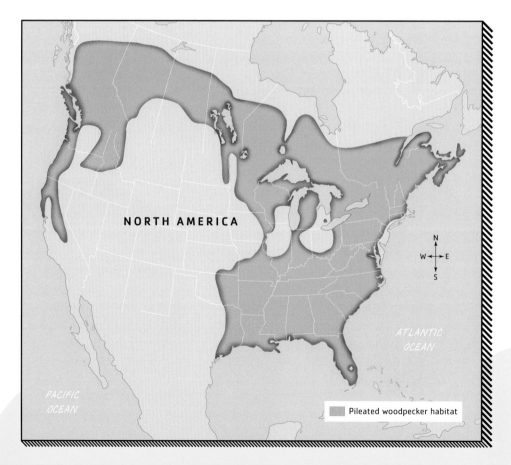

NORTH AMERICA

N
W   E
S

ATLANTIC OCEAN

PACIFIC OCEAN

■ Pileated woodpecker habitat

Pileated woodpeckers live in forests with large, old trees. At night, they sleep in holes in trees that they've dug out for roosting. A pileated woodpecker's habitat often includes a pond or stream. Birds fly to these bodies of water to drink.

A pileated woodpecker pokes its head out of the nest.

PILEATED WOODPECKERS VS. WOOD THRUSHES

Ee-oh-lay! A wood thrush loudly sings while perched in a shrub. Wood thrushes are chunky, reddish-brown birds with spotted necks and undersides. Their habitat is similar to the habitat of pileated woodpeckers.

A wood thrush bathes in a woodland stream.

Wood thrushes live in wooded areas in the eastern United States. Like pileated woodpeckers, they live in forests with tall trees. Wood thrushes also live near a source of water for drinking. They look for forests with moist soil and rotting leaves on the ground. It's here that they find most of their food. Wood thrushes are omnivores, like pileated woodpeckers. Wood thrushes eat fruit and nuts, but they mostly feed on insects.

PILEATED WOODPECKERS VS. CACTUS WRENS

A cactus wren sits atop a prickly cactus, looking out over its desert home. Cactus wrens live in hot, dry habitats with large cactuses, desert bushes, and other thorny desert plants. Cactus wrens rest in the shade of these plants during the hottest part of the day.

Like pileated woodpeckers, cactus wrens are omnivores. They feed mostly on insects that scurry over the desert floor. They also eat berries from desert plants. Unlike pileated woodpeckers, cactus wrens don't live near streams or ponds. They get their water from the food they eat.

Tough skin protects the feet and legs of a cactus wren from cactus spikes.

COMPARE IT!

PILEATED WOODPECKERS

VS.

CACTUS WRENS

Forest ◀ HABITAT ▶ Desert

SOUTHERN CANADA AND THE WESTERN, MIDWESTERN, AND EASTERN UNITED STATES ◀ RANGE ▶ SOUTHWESTERN UNITED STATES AND MEXICO

PONDS AND STREAMS ◀ WATER SOURCE ▶ FRUITS AND INSECTS

CHAPTER 3

PILEATED WOODPECKERS IN ACTION

Little by little, a pileated woodpecker carves out a hole in a rotting tree. When the hole is deep enough, the woodpecker pushes its tongue inside. With the pointed tip of its tongue, it probes for ants and pulls them into its mouth.

A pileated woodpecker uses its powerful neck, head, and beak to drill holes into dead wood. The holes are shaped like rectangles. They can be more than 1 foot (0.3 meters) long. The woodpeckers use their sticky, spear-shaped tongues to search for insects tunneled into the wood.

DID YOU KNOW?

Pileated woodpeckers drill such large feeding holes that they cause some trees to **BREAK** in half.

Pileated woodpeckers live in the same territory all year long. They often share this area with a mate. Together, the pair marks the boundaries of their territory with sound. They drum loudly on trees at the edges of their territory.

PILEATED WOODPECKERS VS. GREAT SPOTTED WOODPECKERS

A great spotted woodpecker clings to the side of a tree. It uses its beak to pry up a piece of bark. Great spotted woodpeckers live in the forests of Europe and Asia. They are smaller than pileated woodpeckers.

Great spotted woodpeckers cling to tree trunks with their legs wide apart. For added support, they press their tail against the tree. Pileated woodpeckers use this same stance to grip trees.

Great spotted woodpeckers peck and pull at the bark of living trees. Their tongues capture insects just below

The male great spotted woodpecker has a red patch on its head, while the female does not.

COMPARE IT!

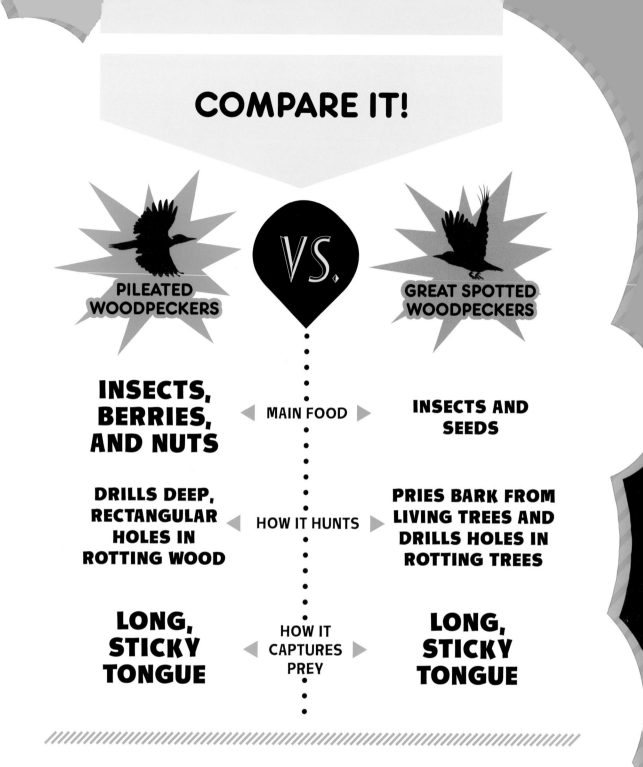

PILEATED WOODPECKERS

VS.

GREAT SPOTTED WOODPECKERS

INSECTS, BERRIES, AND NUTS ◀ MAIN FOOD ▶ **INSECTS AND SEEDS**

DRILLS DEEP, RECTANGULAR HOLES IN ROTTING WOOD ◀ HOW IT HUNTS ▶ **PRIES BARK FROM LIVING TREES AND DRILLS HOLES IN ROTTING TREES**

LONG, STICKY TONGUE ◀ HOW IT CAPTURES PREY ▶ **LONG, STICKY TONGUE**

the bark's surface. Sometimes they dig deep holes in rotting wood to capture insects. Like pileated woodpeckers, great spotted woodpeckers live in the same territory year-round. They share this territory with a mate, and they mark it with a drumming sound.

PILEATED WOODPECKERS VS. SNOW GEESE

Feeding on tall grasses, a snow goose stands at the edge of a marsh. Snow geese are named for their snow-white feathers. They are herbivores. These geese feed on grasses and other plants near lakes, ponds, and marshes. A hungry snow goose yanks an entire plant from the ground and eats every part.

Snow geese are excellent fliers. Unlike pileated woodpeckers, snow geese migrate. They fly thousands of miles to their winter and summer territories. They don't live alone or in pairs the way pileated woodpeckers do. Instead, they live and migrate in large flocks.

Snow geese rest their feet by standing on one leg at a time. They sometimes tuck one foot into their feathers to keep it warm.

Snow geese react differently to predators than pileated woodpeckers do. If a predator such as a hawk or owl comes near a pileated woodpecker, the woodpecker freezes and goes silent. If it is really threatened, it flies away. Snow geese have fewer predators than pileated woodpeckers. Snow geese can outrun many of their predators, but foxes and wolves prey on snow geese eggs.

CHAPTER 4
THE LIFE CYCLE OF PILEATED WOODPECKERS

The life cycle of the pileated woodpecker begins in early spring. Both the male and the female use their beaks to drum loudly on trees to attract a mate. Male and female pileated woodpeckers stay with the same mate for life.

Young pileated woodpeckers

An adult pileated woodpecker feeds chicks in its nest.

Pileated woodpeckers build their nests in holes they dig out of trees. In the nest, a female lays three to five white eggs. Both the male and the female take turns incubating the eggs, which hatch after fifteen to eighteen days. They eat food that the adult woodpeckers regurgitate into their mouths. Pileated woodpecker chicks begin to grow feathers when they are about seven days old.

Young pileated woodpeckers are old enough to leave the nest by twenty-eight days. They follow their parents around for two to three months. During this time, they learn how to find insects and avoid predators. The young pileated woodpeckers reach adulthood the following spring, in time for the next mating season. Pileated woodpeckers live for about ten years.

PILEATED WOODPECKERS VS. EASTERN SCREECH OWLS

An eastern screech owl roosts in a tree hole, blending in perfectly with the tree bark. Eastern screech owls are named for their call, which sounds like a ghostly screech. Like pileated woodpeckers, male and female eastern screech owls mate for life. Both birds also use tree holes as nests. Eastern screech owls use old woodpecker nests or natural holes in trees.

Female eastern screech owls lay two to five eggs, which hatch after twenty-seven to thirty-four days. Like young pileated woodpeckers, the young eastern screech owls leave their nest after about a month. They stay with their parents for at least two more months. During that time, the young owls slowly learn to hunt. They are fully grown and ready to mate after one year. Eastern screech owls live for about ten years in the wild.

Baby owls are covered in fuzzy down that is replaced by feathers as they grow.

COMPARE IT!

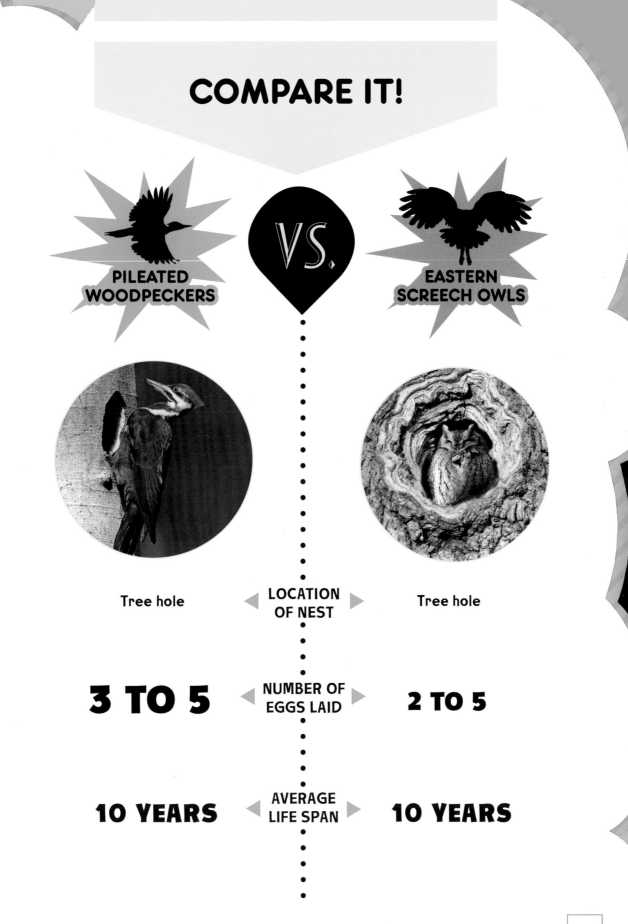

PILEATED WOODPECKERS

VS.

EASTERN SCREECH OWLS

Tree hole — LOCATION OF NEST — Tree hole

3 TO 5 — NUMBER OF EGGS LAID — **2 TO 5**

10 YEARS — AVERAGE LIFE SPAN — **10 YEARS**

PILEATED WOODPECKERS VS. BROWN PELICANS

A brown pelican flies high over the ocean. Tucking its head into its body, it zooms down to catch a fish. Brown pelicans spend most of their lives on coasts near the ocean. When it's time to mate, they go to islands that are safe from predators such as foxes. Brown pelicans build nests of grasses and other soft plants, either in a tree or on the ground.

A young brown pelican is covered with white feathers. It will grow brown feathers by the time it's an adult.

Brown pelicans incubate their eggs by standing on them with their warm, webbed feet. The eggs hatch about one month later. By three months, brown pelican chicks are ready to set off on their own. They are ready to mate in three or four years, compared to just one year for pileated woodpeckers. Brown pelicans can live more than twenty-five years.

Adult pelicans vomit digested food that is easy for chicks to eat, right from the bill!

PILEATED WOODPECKER TRAIT CHART

This book explores pileated woodpeckers and the ways they are similar to and different from other birds. What other birds would you like to learn about?

	WARM-BLOODED	FEATHERS ON BODY	LAYS HARD-SHELLED EGGS	SPONGY SKULL BONE	OMNIVORE	NESTS IN TREE HOLES
PILEATED WOODPECKER	X	X	X	X	X	X
GREATER ROADRUNNER	X	X	X		X	
AMERICAN FLAMINGO	X	X	X		X	
WOOD THRUSH	X	X	X		X	
CACTUS WREN	X	X	X		X	
GREAT SPOTTED WOODPECKER	X	X	X	X	X	X
SNOW GOOSE	X	X	X			
EASTERN SCREECH OWL	X	X	X			X
BROWN PELICAN	X	X	X			

beak: the jaws and mouth of a bird. Beaks are sometimes called bills, especially when they are long and flat.

chisel: a long metal tool used for chipping, carving, and cutting into a solid material

crest: a tuft of feathers, fur, or skin sticking up from an animal's head

flocks: groups of birds in a particular place that belong to one species

habitats: environments where animals naturally live. A habitat is the place where an animal can find food, water, air, shelter, and a place to raise its young.

herbivores: plant-eating animals

incubating: sitting or standing on eggs to keep them warm. Only eggs kept at a safe temperature will hatch.

larvae: young wormlike forms (such as grubs or caterpillars) that hatch from the eggs of various kinds of insects

migrate: to move from one area or habitat to another. Animals migrate to seek warmer or cooler climates or to find more plentiful prey.

omnivores: animals that eat both plants and meat

predators: animals that hunt, or prey on, other animals

prey: an animal that is hunted and killed by a predator for food

regurgitate: to bring swallowed food back up into the mouth

roosting: settling down to rest or sleep

species: animals that share common features and can produce offspring

territory: an area that is occupied and defended by an animal or a group of animals

traits: features that are inherited from parents. Body size and feather color are examples of inherited traits.

wingspan: the length of a bird's wings from the tip of one wing to the tip of the other

LERNER

Expand learning beyond the printed book. Download free, complementary educational resources for this book from our website, www.lernersource.com.

SOURCE

SELECTED BIBLIOGRAPHY

Alsop, Fred J., III. *Smithsonian Birds of North America*. New York: DK, 2001.

Bull, Evelyn L., and Jerome A. Jackson. "Pileated Woodpecker: *Dryocopus pileatus*." *The Birds of North America*, no. 148. Last modified September 27, 2011. http://bna.birds.cornell.edu/bna /species/148/articles/introduction.

Harrison, Colin, and Alan Greensmith. *Birds of the World*. New York: DK, 1993.

"Pileated Woodpecker: *Dryocopus pileatus*." The Cornell Lab of Ornithology. Accessed March 30, 2015. http://www .allaboutbirds.org/guide/Pileated_ Woodpecker/lifehistory.

Young, Diana. "*Dryocopus pileatus*: Pileated Woodpecker." *Animal Diversity Web*. Last modified May 22, 2003. http:// animaldiversity.org/accounts /Dryocopus_pileatus/.

FURTHER INFORMATION

Defenders of Wildlife: Woodpeckers
http://www.defenders.org/woodpeckers /basic-facts
Find out what traits woodpeckers have in common.

Johnson, Jinny. *Animal Planet™ Atlas of Animals*. Minneapolis: Millbrook Press, 2012. Travel around the world and explore the planet's incredible animal diversity in this richly illustrated book.

National Geographic: Pileated Woodpecker
http://video.nationalgeographic.com /video/woodpecker_pileated
Watch a video of pileated woodpeckers in action.

National Geographic Kids: Pileated Woodpecker
http://kids.nationalgeographic.com /content/kids/en_US/animals/pileated -woodpecker
Visit this *National Geographic* website for pileated woodpecker facts and photos.

Riggs, Kate. *Woodpeckers*. Mankato, MN: Creative Education, 2014. Learn about the appearance, habitat, behavior, and life cycle of different kinds of woodpeckers.

INDEX